# COOKING IN THE YOUNG REPUBLIC 1780-1850

Patricia B. Mitchell

*Published 1992 by the author at the Sims-Mitchell House Bed & Breakfast, 242 Whittle Street SW, P. O. Box 429, Chatham, VA 2453l (telephone 804-432- 0595, fax 804-432-0596).*

*Printed in the U. S. A.*
*ISBN 0-925117-57-9*

*Fourth Printing, April 1995*

**To the Reader:**

*If there is a particular recipe for which you are looking, please write me at the above address and I will try to find it for you. If you have recipes which you would like to share, I would love to receive them.*

*- Patricia B. Mitchell*

# TABLE OF CONTENTS

# INTRODUCTION

A daring concept, a bold experiment -- that of creating a large, self-governing body of states melded into one union. Many of the founders of this country came here in search of liberty: religious, economic, and social. Would a strong central government jeopardize this hard-won freedom? Would having a president turn this somewhat governmentally unstructured group of states into a parody of a monarchy in which liberties could be capriciously denied?

Wise men gambled on the chance that their concept of an acceptable form of government would work. As elderly Benjamin Franklin left the 1787 Constitutional Convention in Philadelphia it is said that a woman walked over to him and asked, "What kind of government has been formed?" His answer was, "A republic, if you can keep it!" [1]

In this new republic, elected representatives would serve the people, reflecting the opinions and desires of the majority. The success of this self-governing plan was based upon the confidence that the representatives would vote with the best interests of the masses in mind; and that the representatives would not fall prey to selfish aims such as the pursuit of personal power and profit. The leaders were expected to be of a high moral caliber. The epitome of this type of person was demonstrated in the new country's choice of president -- George Washington. Other luminaries included John Adams, Thomas Jefferson, James Madison, and James Monroe, men whose names were already written in history as a result of their leadership roles in the period of the American Revolution. Dolley Madison, too, won a place in the books and hearts of Americans, as did rough and ready Daniel Boone, and the dashing Andrew Jackson.

In this period around 1780 to 1850, another cast of characters, too, was performing, but not in the political arena. These were a new breed: American women who wrote cookbooks. These ladies are not as well-known now, but many of the food trends they recorded and helped to promote are as prominent in current American life as are governmental ideas and actions set in motion by the leaders of the young republic. The purpose of this book is to gather together in a sort of ***bouquet garni*** historical facts about people and events of the day, and recipes showing what was cooking -- in the culinary sense of the phrase.

The Americans' conflict with England during the American Revolution and the War of 1812 caused English styles -- including food styles -- to fall from favor noticeably. The French alliance of the Revolution, the Marquis de Lafayette's status as a national hero, and the import of French culture by American diplomats (Thomas Jefferson, especially) were factors which moved upper-class foodstyles markedly toward the French -- a trend which reached its peak later, during the lavish stylistic opulence of the Victorian era.

In the meantime, at the frontier and subsistence levels of the economy, indigenous foods, game, and easily-cared-for domestic animals provided the basis for an "American country cooking" which to this day echoes the influences not only of English settlers, but also of West Africans, Germans, Scots, provincial Frenchmen, Native Americans, and others who so ably lived off the American land.

During this age, in the North, industrial entrepreneurs began to acquire vast fortunes from the efforts of factory labor. In the South, landed gentry moved into a gilded era made possible by profits from slave labor. In the West, farmers and ranchers worked to tame the land. And overall, steamboats and railroads began to physically knit the nation together, making possible divisions of labor between farm and factory, city and country; and thus facilitating for the first time large-scale food production and distribution.

In all the hubbub, the cooking pot was becoming a melting pot. The food of the young republic was in the process of becoming distinctively American.

# Chapter 1

# "New" Foods Documented

Up until the late 1700's, American homemakers relied upon English cookbooks such as E. Smith's ***The Compleat Housewife or Accomplish'd Gentlewoman's Companion*** which appeared in both London and Williamsburg editions in 1742;[2] Hannah Glasse's ***The Art of Cookery Made Plain and Easy*** published in London in 1747; and Susannah Carter's ***The Frugal Housewife*** published in Boston in 1772. (Mrs. Carter's first edition contains plates on carving by Paul Revere.) The first important cookbook written and published in the United States was Amelia Simmons' ***American Cookery***. This work, penned by an "orphan," as Ms. Simmons describes herself, appeared on April 28, 1796, in Hartford, Connecticut. It was printed by Hudson and Goodwin and the complete title was: ***American Cookery, or the Art of Dressing Viands, Fish, Poultry and Vegetables, and the Best Modes of Making Pastes, Puffs, Pies, Tarts, Puddings, Custards and Preserves, and All Kinds of Cakes, from the Imperial Plumb to Plain Cake. Adapted to this Country, and All Grades of Life. By Amelia Simmons, an American Orphan***.[3]

The cookbook was a success, and the demand for Ms. Simmons' writing was so great that she soon found herself "under a necessity of publishing a second edition." She did so around 1800.[4]

What captured the public's fancy were Ms. Simmons' recipes utilizing native foods such as pumpkin, "Indian meal" (cornmeal), and maple syrup (recipes which were not, of course, included in English cookbooks of the day.)[5]

Ms. Simmons' book contained traditional English recipes such as instructions on the preparation of meat pies, syllabubs, trifles, pound cakes, and Shrewsbury Cake, but she also offered her readers directions for "Crookneck of

Winter Squash Pudding." The vegetable itself as well as its Native American (Algonquian) - derived name was definitely American. "Squash" comes from "askootasquash" -- literally, "eaten raw." The authoress' advice to add dried whortleberries (similar to blueberries or huckleberries) to enhance the pudding also reflects an Indian practice.[6]

Other innovative recipes included boiled and baked Indian Puddings, Johny Cake or Hoe Cake, and Indian Slapjacks (all using cornmeal); a pumpkin pie much like those served today; and an apple pudding akin to our modern apple pie in that the recipe calls for sliced apples, rather than the traditional stewed and strained apples. Ms. Simmons also promoted the use of pearlash (refined potash -- potassium carbonate -- derived from wood ashes) as a quick leavening agent in cookies and cakes. This precursor of baking powder was a revolutionary ingredient, unknown in England at the time.[7] Its use enabled Ms. Simmons and her readers to make soft gingerbread (like cake) rather than the old-fashioned plank-like crisp ginger cookies and cakes. (Up to this time baked goods were leavened with beaten eggs, or yeast, or sour milk and molasses, or alcoholic spirits.)

The "American orphan" foodwriter referred to molasses by its American name, rather than using the British term "treacle." She spoke of "emptins" (semi-liquid prepared yeast); "slapjack" for a cake fried on a griddle; "shortning" or "shortening" for fats. She used the Dutch word "cooky" for "little cake," and "slaw" for "salad," well before lexicographer Webster recognized them.[8] [Later during the federal period Washington Irving, author of "Rip Van Winkle" and "The Legend of Sleepy Hollow" wrote mouth-watering descriptions of Dutch food. In his ***Knickerbocker's History of New York*** he speaks of "immense apple pies," "saucers full of preserved peaches and pears," and "an enormous dish of balls of sweetened dough, fried in hog's fat, and called doughnuts or olykoeks . . ."][9]

This first national cookbook gives recipes for American Citron (watermelon rind pickle); and her second edition contains recipes for Federal Pan Cake, Independence, and Election Cake. Ms. Simmons documents the popular "rye 'n' injun" (rye flour and cornmeal) bread, and "chouder" (chowder).[10] She suggests serving cranberry sauce with roast turkey; using corn cobs in smoking bacon; and brewing the popular spruce beer, a drink recipe served in Europe and America but never published before. (After ***American Cooking*** appeared, new editions of English cookbooks also intended for sale in the United States contained recipes for foods which Ms. Simmons had first presented.)

***American Cookery*** mentions the North American Jerusalem artichoke and recommends numerous vegetables and herbs to cultivate in the American garden. She expresses her opinion about garlic, "Garlicks, tho' used by the French, are better adapted to the uses of medicine than cookery." [11] About parsley she points out, "a pleasurably tasted herb, and much used in garnishing viands." [12] She frowns slightly upon sage, remarking, "Sage is used in Cheese and Pork, but not generally approved." [13]

Ms. Simmons also offered housewifely "tips" on foods, as in the manner of other cookbooks of the day. She explained how to check eggs for freshness (they ought not float!);[14] the desirability of pea hens for cooking rather than the "tough, hard, stringy, and untasted, and even indelicious . . . tho' beautifully plummaged" peacock;[15] and the secret of keeping green peas "'til Christmas" (dried, and placed with mutton suet in a bottle which was corked and then covered and tied with a bladder and leather).[16] She presented this rather intriguing advice about salmon:

> *"**Salmon**, the noblest and richest fish taken in fresh water -- the largest are the best. They are unlike almost every other fish, are ameliorated [improved] by being 3 or 4 days out of water, if kept from heat and the moon, which has much more injurious effect than the sun.*

*"In all great fish-markets, great fish-mongers strictly examine the gills -- if the bright redness is exchanged for a low brown, they are stale; but when live fish are bro't flouncing into market, you have only to elect the kind most agreeable to your palate and the season."* [17]

Ms. Simmons knew better than to overcook string beans:

***"TO BOIL FRENCH BEANS"***

*"Take your beans and string them, cut in two and then across, when you have done them all, sprinkle them over with salt, stir them together, as soon as your water boils put them in and make them boil up quick, they will be soon done and they will look of a better green than when growing in the garden if; they are very young, only break off the ends, the[n] break in two and dress them in the same manner."* [18]

Following are two of Ms. Simmons' previously-mentioned thoroughly-American recipes.

***"THE AMERICAN CITRON"***

*"Take the rine [rind] of a large watermelon not too ripe, cut it into small pieces, take two pound of loaf sugar, one pint of water, put it all into a kettle, let it boil gently for four hours, then put it into pots for use."* [19]

***"A CROOKNECK, OR WINTER SQUASH PUDDING"***

*"Core, boil and skin a good squash, and bruize [bruise] it well; take 6 large apples, pared, cored, and stewed tender, mix together; add 6 or 7 spoonsful of dry bread or biscuit, rendered fine as meal, half pint milk or cream, 2 spoons of*

*rose-water, 2 do. ["do." means "ditto" -- in this case 2 spoons] wine, 5 or 6 eggs beaten and strained, nutmeg, salt and sugar to your taste, one spoon flour, beat all smartly together, bake.*

*"The above is a good receipt for Pompkins, Potatoes or Yams, adding more moistening or milk and rose water, and to the two latter a few black or Lisbon currants, or dry whortleberries scattered in, will make it better."* [20]

Shrewsbury Cakes are flat, round biscuit-like cakes which were a specialty of Shrewsbury in Shropshire, England.[21]

### *"SHREWSBURY CAKE"*

*"One pound butter, three quarters of a pound sugar, a little mace, four eggs mixed and beat with your hand, till very light, put the composition to one pound flour, roll into small cakes -- bake with a light oven."* [22] *[Note: Bake at 400° F.]*

The following is one of Ms. Simmons' traditional crispy-type gingerbread recipes, followed by two more modern (soft) versions.

### *GINGERBREAD "NO. 4"*

*"Three pounds sugar, half pound butter, quarter of a pound of ginger, one doz. eggs, one glass rose water, rub into three pounds flour. [Knead it stiff, shape it to your fancy, bake 15 minutes.]"* [23]

### *MOLASSES GINGERBREAD*

*1 egg*
*1/2 c. granulated sugar*

*1/2 c. molasses*
*1 c. sour milk*
*1/4 c. fat*
*2 c. soft wheat or pastry flour*
*3/4 tsp. baking soda*
*1/2 tsp. salt*
*3/4 tsp. ginger*
*1 tsp. cinnamon*
*1/2 tsp. nutmeg*
*2 tsp. baking powder*

*"Sift some flour; then measure it. Add the leavening and spices.*

*"In a mixing bowl, beat the egg. Add the sugar, molasses, and sour milk, and mix well. Melt the fat; add it to the egg mixture.*

*"Add the dry ingredients to the egg mixture, passing them through a sifter while adding them. Beat until all ingredients are well mixed. Pour into a greased pan. A 9-inch square pan is suitable for this recipe. Bake in a moderate oven -- 350° F. -- for 35 to 40 minutes or until the cake is sufficiently baked. . . . Yield: 16 pieces, about 2 inches square."*[24]

## *MAMA'S MODERN HEALTH GINGERBREAD*

*2 c. whole wheat flour*
*1 tsp. soda*
*2 tsp. ginger and 1 tsp. cinnamon, or 1 tbsp. ginger*
*1/4 tsp. nutmeg*
*1/4 tsp. salt*
*1/3 c. sugar*
*2 tbsp. oil*
*1 1/3 c. hot milk*
*1/3 c. molasses*

*Combine dry ingredients. Pour in liquids. Stir and spoon into a greased 9-inch square pan. Bake at 350° F. for 25-30 minutes. Serve with a sauce (lemon, for example).*

### *LEMON SAUCE*

*1/3 c. sugar*
*2 tbsp. cornstarch*
*1/8 tsp. salt*
*1 c. water*

*1/3 c. lemon juice*
*2 tsp. grated lemon zest (optional)*

*Combine the first four ingredients in a small saucepan. Cook until thickened, stirring frequently. Add lemon juice, and warm. Serve warm with hot or cold (room temperature) gingerbread or cake.*

The next recipe is said to have been the one which George Washington's mother prepared for the French hero of the American Revolution, the Marquis de Lafayette, when he unexpectedly came to visit her in Fredericksburg, Virginia, in 1784 during his return trip to America. With the spicy gingerbread Mrs. Washington served mint juleps. As they enjoyed the refreshments Lafayette kept praising General Washington. Mrs. Washington only remarked, "George was always a good boy."

### *"LAFAYETTE GINGER BREAD"*

*"Cut up in a pan 1/2 cup of the very best fresh butter with 1/2 cup of excellent brown sugar, beat to a cream with a paddle. Add 1 cup of West India molasses and 1/2 cup of warm milk; 2 tablespoons of powdered ginger and 1 heaping teaspoon of cinnamon, mace and nutmeg powdered and mixed; 1 wine glass of brandy (I use coffee now). Beat 3*

*eggs till very light and thick; 3 cups of flour and 1 teaspoon of cream of tartar sifted with flour and stirred alternately with the beaten eggs into the batter. Last, mix in the juice and grated rind of 1 large orange. Dissolve 1 teaspoon of soda in a little warm water, and stir in. Beat until very light. A cup full of seeded raisins is an addition. Bake in a loaf, sheet or patty pans, in a moderate oven."* [26]

Note: Ms. Simmons and other cooks in the young republic prepared food by the open fireplace or in a brick oven. Cooking stoves were not known until about 1840 and then were not owned by many average people until around 1900.[26]

# Chapter 2

# Food of the Famous

Rivals of Thomas Jefferson during the 1800 presidential campaign claimed that the Virginian was unqualified since he had been "raised wholly on hoe-cake made of coarse-ground Southern corn, bacon and hominy." Ironically enough, it was Jefferson who introduced many European foods to this country, as well as serving American foodstuffs to Europeans while he resided there as foreign minister.[27] Jefferson's openness to new food ideas; endless experimentation in animal and plant husbandry as well as food preparation; and his Herculean accomplishment as a host, over his lifetime, of thousands in his own home qualify him for the title, "Father of His Country's Cuisine."

In 1784 Jefferson joined John Adams and Benjamin Franklin as minister plenipotentiary to negotiate treaties of amity and commerce in Europe. At the time of his appointment Jefferson wrote William Short, who was to become his private secretary, "I propose for a particular purpose to carry my servant James [Hemings] with me [to France]." Hemings had been functioning as a house servant, messenger, and occasionally a driver for Jefferson up to that point.

In the summer of 1784 Thomas Jefferson, his daughter Martha, and James Hemings set sail from Boston for Europe, arriving in France by August 1. Here James began to prepare for the "particular purpose" Jefferson had in mind by studying cooking with a restaurant keeper named Combeaux.[28]

In late 1786 or early 1787 he had advanced in cooking skills enough to begin to learn pastry making. He had mastered the French language and then received further cooking instruction at, according to Jefferson, "great expense" from one of the prince di Conde's cooks. In 1787 James assumed the duties of *chef de cuisine* (head chef) at the Hotel de Langeac, Jefferson's Parisian residence. James was paid twenty livres per week.[29]

When Jefferson, his daughter, and James returned from France, James became *chef de cuisine* at Monticello, and went with Jefferson to New York when Jefferson served as secretary of state. When the capital was moved to Philadelphia, James assumed the role of overseeing the kitchen at Jefferson's home at 287 High Street (now Market Street).

In 1796 Jefferson freed James, but prior to that Jefferson required that James return to Monticello and teach "such a person as I shall place under him for the purpose to be a good cook." James trained his brother Peter, a "servant of great intelligence and diligence," as Monticello's *chef de cuisine* and resident brewmaster.[30]

Always thorough, before James left Monticello to go out on his own he compiled a well-written "Inventory of kitchen utensils."[31] Obviously this highly-educated man had fulfilled in all respects Jefferson's "particular [culinary] purpose."

Jefferson enjoyed home cooking, but his sophisticated palate enabled him to appreciate many new recipes, too. Bacon, Jefferson's overseer, commented that "[Jefferson] was never a great eater, but what he did eat he wanted to be very choice."[32] He enjoyed simple fare with an emphasis on vegetables. He was extremely fond of salads, and he wanted to produce olive oil in this country. As a substitute for olive trees (which could not tolerate the Virginia mountain climate), he experimented with sesame (benne) seeds, which can be crushed to make oil.[33]

He also provided his chefs with imported Parmesan cheese. He had observed with his usual keen interest the Italian technique for making genuine Parmesan cheese while traveling in Parma, Italy before he became President.[34] (In 1787 Jefferson had risked the death penalty in Italy by smuggling out a small quantity of rice. That rice revived the Carolina rice industry which had been decimated during the American Revolution by the British army, which shipped the entire rice crop to England, leaving no seed.)[35]

Ever the risk-taking agronomist, Jefferson later found himself in political hot water as the War of 1812 loomed. He was accused of consorting with the enemy because of his letters to, and replies from, London. Needless to say, Jefferson was no traitor. The letters were correspondence with the Board of Agriculture concerning chicory seeds which Jefferson wanted.[36]

At Monticello he devoted much attention to his gardens and orchards and was knowledgeable about herbs. An 1809 letter from Jefferson's correspondent Gen. John Mason reported, "[The tarragon plant] has flourished well in the open air -- and will in Spring afford plenty of slips."[37]

Earlier Jefferson had become known as "the hog governor" because he developed new breeds of pigs by crossing local hogs with some strains from Calcutta.[38] During the 1800 campaign Jefferson's political supporters originated the practice of hosting big barbecues and planning parades to honor their candidate and win votes.[39] The effort was successful and Jefferson became our third president. He received a 1600-pound block of New England cheese in 1801. It was transported to Washington by sleigh, and was still being enjoyed by White House guests in 1803.[40]

White House visitors also ate meals such as this, recorded by Manasseh Cutler on February 6, 1802: " . . . rice soup, round of beef, turkey, mutton, ham, loin of veal, cutlets of veal, fried eggs, fried beef, and 'a pie called macaroni.' Desserts followed. 'Ice cream very good, crust wholly dried, crumbled into thin flakes; a dish somewhat like a pudding -- inside white as milk or curd, very porous and light, covered with cream sauce -- very fine. Many other jim cracks, a great variety of fruit, plenty of wine, and good.'"[41]

In addition to such lavish repasts replete with French sauces and numerous wines, Jefferson personally liked greens, corn on the cob, sweet potatoes, fried apples, battercakes, and other simple food. He even brought his governess up to Washington from Monticello to be sure that his favorite "batter cakes, fried apples and hot breads served with bacon and eggs" were prepared for breakfast.[42] However (according to Louise Conway Belden in ***The Festive Tradition***, "crowded elaborate tables had been a mark of status in England since the early fifteenth century when the king and the princes of the church had vied with each other to demonstrate their wealth and power. The aristocracy . . . copied royalty and nobility . . . wealthy merchants and lesser folk aped the aristocracy. As a result . . . throughout the centuries, a great display of food and a rich setting for it had been a measure of man's position in society."[43] Isaac, a slave at Monticello, recalled, "They would always be a great many carriages coming to Monticello. [Ex-President Jefferson] would never have less than eight covers [places set] at dinner . . . plenty of wine, best old Antigua rum and cider; very fond of cider. [I] never heard of his being disguised in drink [inebriated]." Monticello overseer Edmund Bacon reported that visitors came "in gangs and they almost ate him out of house and home . . . I have killed a fine beef and it would all be eaten in a day or two. There was no tavern in all that country that had so much company."[44] As many as fifty unexpected overnight guests were known to arrive at one time.[45]

One guest, George Tichnor, described a typical day at Monticello in February 1815, beginning with a nine o'clock breakfast of braised partridges, bacon, capitolade of fowl on toast, eggs, cold meats, fried apples, hot breads, battercakes [pancakes], and tansy pudding. Dinner was eaten at 4 p.m. and "was always choice and served in the French style, but no wine was set on the table till the cloth was removed. The ladies sat until about six, then retired, but returned with the tea tray a little before seven, and spent the evening with the gentlemen . . . ."[46]

In maintaining this tradition Jefferson overspent his salary as president and depleted his financial resources in retirement.[47] -- To sample some Jeffersonian-era cuisine, try the following recipes from an 1820's cookbook entitled ***The Virginia Housewife***, by Mary Randolph, "a contemporary of Jefferson's and of the same social milieu."[48]

### *"RICE WOFFLES [WAFFLES]"*

*Thomas Jefferson bought a waffle iron while in Holland so that he could enjoy the crisp batter cakes at home.*

* * *

*"Boil two gills of rice quite soft, mix with it three gills of flour, a little salt, two ounces of melted butter, two eggs beaten well, and as much milk as will make it a thick batter -- beat it till very light, and bake it in woffle irons."*[49]

*Note: One gill equals 1/2 cup.*

Salsify is a plant with long, white- or black-skinned, fleshy roots which have an oysterlike flavor. (In fact, sometimes it is called oyster plant.) The tender leafy tops can be cooked or eaten raw in tossed salads. The root can be steamed, then sliced, battered, and fried to create "mock oysters."

### *"SALSIFY"*

*"Scrape and wash the roots, put them into boiling water with salt; when done drain them in the dish without cutting them up. They are a very excellent vegetable, but require nicety in cooking; exposure to the air, either in scraping or after boiling, will make them black."* [50]

### *"RED BEET ROOTS"*

*"Are not so much used as they deserve to be; they are dressed in the same way as parsnips, only neither scraped nor cut 'till after they are boiled; -- they will take from an hour and a half to three hours in boiling, according to their size; to be sent to the table with salt fish, boiled beef, &c. When young, small and juicy, it is a very good variety, an excellent garnish, and easily converted into a very cheap and pleasant pickle."* [51]

### *"GOOSEBERRY FOOL"*

*Thomas Jefferson enjoyed entertaining guests for dinner, sometimes serving as many as a dozen desserts at what he called his "sinful feasts." His dessert table included sweets such as blancmange, meringue, and macaroons. (Thomas Jefferson called Floating Island, a French dessert, "snow eggs.") Mary Randolph included the following sweet fruit puree known as Gooseberry Fool in the 1824 edition of her cookbook:*

* * *

*"Pick the stems and blossoms from two quarts of green gooseberries. Put them in a stewpan with their weight in loaf sugar and a very little water; when sufficiently stewed, pass the pulp through a sieve, and when cold, add rich boiled custard till it is like thick cream. Put it in a glass bowl and lay the frothed cream on the top."*[52]

*Note: A gooseberry is a sour berry which resembles a currant but is a little larger.*

Ms. Randolph had sound advice for pudding and cake preparation:

> *". . . Before a pudding or cake is begun, every ingredient necessary for it must be ready; when the process is retarded by neglecting to have them prepared the article is injured. The oven must be in a proper state . . . . Promptitude is necessary in all our actions, but never moreso than when engaged in making cakes or puddings . . . ."* [53]

Besides being credited with being "one of the best cooks in America," Mary Randolph helped to influence future eating trends by documenting favorite American dishes like pigs' feet, catfish soup, and hominy. Her book reflects the influence of French, English, Spanish, Creole, and Native American cookery on the nation's diet, as the United States emerged as a cultural melting pot.[54]

Ms. Randolph's work also presents recipes for beaten biscuit; shoat (young pig); fourteen recipes using tomatoes including a recipe for tomato catsup (the first time this fruit appeared in an American cookbook); recipes calling for okra and eggplant; and "an ordinate number of fine recipes for ice cream." [55] ***The Virginia Housewife*** also demonstrates the strong influence of black culinary skills, black women often having been the cooks for the wealthy.[56]

In addition, Ms. Randolph offered words of wisdom:

*"The government of a family bears a Lilliputian resemblance to the government of a nation."* [57]

*"Profusion is not elegance -- a dinner justly calculated for the company, and consisting for the greater part of small articles, correctly prepared, and neatly served up, will make a much more pleasing appearance to the sight, and give a far greater gratification to the appetite, than a table loaded with food, and from the multiplicity of dishes, unavoidably neglected in the preparation, and served up cold."* [58]

The following recipes reflect the influence of Ms. Randolph's cooking style.

## *CLIVEDEN WAFFLES*

*3 eggs, separated*
*1 tsp. sugar*
*2 c. milk*
*2 c. flour*
*1/2 tsp. salt*
*1/4 c. melted butter*

*"Beat egg whites in large mixer bowl until soft peaks form; add sugar and beat to stiff peaks. Set aside. Beat yolks; add milk, flour and salt to yolks and mix just enough to blend. Stir melted butter into yolk mixture with mixer on low speed. Fold into egg whites; blend thoroughly. Bake in hot waffle iron. Yield: three 9-inch waffles."* [59]

## *"NAPLES BISCUITS"*

*4 egg whites*
*1/2 tsp. salt*

*1 c. sugar*
*4 egg yolks*
*3 tsp. vanilla or rose water*
*1 1/2 c. sifted flour*
*Powdered sugar (optional)*

*"Beat egg whites and salt until soft peaks form; gradually add sugar and continue beating until sugar is dissolved. Add unbeaten egg yolks, one at a time, beating after each addition. Stir in vanilla or rose water. Lightly fold in flour. Place brown paper on a cookie sheet; spoon dough into finger-shaped mounds on paper (use teaspoon to push dough off side of tablespoon). Place mounds two inches apart to allow for spreading. Bake at 350° F. for 15 minutes. Remove from paper and place on cooling rack. If desired, sprinkle with powdered sugar. Yield: 4 dozen biscuits.*

*"Note: These are sweet tea biscuits similar to ladyfingers."* [60]

### *"CHOCOLATE BLANC MANGE"*

*"Soak 1 pkg. gelatin in one cup of milk. Place on stove 1 3/4 cakes chocolate. Melt and add 1/2 cup sugar, into this stir 6 cups of milk.*

*"When hot, pour mixture over six well beaten egg yolks with 1/2 cup sugar. Return to stove and let thicken -- stirring constantly. When thick, add gelatin. Cook a little longer and if necessary, strain.*

*"Flavor with a little vanilla and a bit of salt. When cold and very thick, add the six egg whites, beaten stiffly.*

*"Pour in well-rinsed bowl -- do not dry bowl. Serve with whipped cream."* [61]

### *"MERINGUES"*

*4 egg whites*
*1 1/2 c. sugar*

*2 tsp. vinegar*
*2 tsp. vanilla*
*2 tsp. cornstarch*

*"Preheat oven to 450° F. Beat egg whites with all ingredients but sugar until soft peaks form. Add sugar gradually until it is dissolved. Put spoonfuls of mixture on brown paper on cookie sheet. Build up sides slightly if meringues are to be filled [with, for example, ice cream or whipped cream]. Put in oven, turn it off and leave meringues for 2-3 hours. Makes about 2 dozen 3-inch meringues."* [62]

## *"SALSIFY SOUP"*

*"Wash and scrape your salsify. To 1/2 doz. good-sized stalks, I allow the breast of a chicken or a leg and a wing. Cover with water and let boil till the meat comes from the bone and the salsify is perfectly soft. Then strain and return liquor to saucepan. To two cups liquor allow 1 cup fresh milk, a little butter, salt and pepper and 1 egg well beaten. Boil all well together. This is as I prepare it for a sick person. For the table it calls for 1 qt. of milk to 2 qts. liquor, 2 eggs, and seasoning to taste."* [63]

## *STEWED TOMATOES*

*2 c. canned, or 3 to 5 peeled and diced fresh tomatoes*
*1-3 tsp. honey or sugar*
*Salt and pepper to taste*
*1 tbsp. butter or margarine*
*2 slices dry whole wheat bread (preferably homemade)*

*Simmer the tomatoes about 10 minutes. Add the seasonings. Meanwhile cube or crumble the bread into a serving bowl. Pour the tomato mixture over the bread and serve.*

Our second president, John Adams, was not known as a gourmet. He contrasted the foodways of his administration and Jefferson's: "I dined a large company once or twice a week. Jefferson dined a dozen every day. I held levees [parties] once a week. Jefferson's whole eight years was a levee."[64]

Jefferson's successor James Madison had a belle of a wife, Dolley. She was a charming and lovable hostess, fond of people and entertaining. Ice cream was first served at the White House when Dolley was acting as Thomas Jefferson's hostess.[65] (Jefferson himself introduced a complex 18-step recipe for a frozen dessert with pastry crust which resembled modern Baked Alaska, which has already been mentioned.)

Dolley Madison served strawberry ice cream (made with fresh cream from the Madison's dairy and fresh strawberries from Dolly's garden[66] ) at President Madison's second inaugural banquet in 1812, but this novel dessert was already making "political raves" in 1789 when Mrs. Alexander Hamilton served it at a dinner attended by George Washington. The next summer Washington bought over $200 worth of ice cream from a New York shop, and subsequently bought a "cream machine for making ice" to use at Mount Vernon.[67] He also owned "two pewter ice cream pots."[68]

### *DOLLEY'S ICE CREAM*

*4 c. milk*
*8 eggs, separated*
*4 c. sugar*
*6 c. cream*
*1 tsp. vanilla*

*Heat the milk almost to boiling. Beat the egg yolks and add the sugar, mixing well. Gradually add the hot milk. Beat the egg white and fold them in. Using a double boiler cook the mixture, stirring until thick. Pour into a bowl and allow to cool. Beat in the cream and vanilla. Pour this custard mixture into an ice cream freezer container. Pack ice cubes and salt around the container. Cover. Allow it to chill for an hour and then beat the custard until smooth. Cover again and freeze another three hours or longer. Take container out of the ice cream freezer. Wrap a towel wrung out with boiling water around the container and slip out the ice cream.*[69]

One Dolley dinner was described by an enchanted guest:

> *"Last night I was bid by our President to the White House, and it was a most unusual affair. Mrs. Madison always entertains with Grace and Charm, but last night there was a sparkle in her eye that set astir an Air of Expectancy among her Guests. When finally the brilliant Assemblage -- America's best -- entered the dining room, they beheld a Table set with French china and English silver, laden with good things to eat, and in the Centre high on a sliver platter, a large shining dome of pink Ice Cream."* [70]

With ice cream you may wish to serve tea cakes (what we call cookies).

### *GREAT-GREAT-GREAT GRANDMOTHER'S TEA CAKES*

*4 c. plain flour*
*2 c. sugar (white)*
*2 eggs*
*1/2 lb. butter*
*2 tbsp. sweet milk*
*1 tsp. cream of tartar*
*1 tsp. ground nutmeg*

*Sift soda and cream of tartar with flour. Beat eggs, add sugar, and beat again. Add milk and flavor with ground nutmeg.*

*Work butter into flour and other ingredients and work all together.*

*The dough will be soft -- so you need to flour the board -- and flour the portion of dough to be rolled out. Roll dough thin -- cut with small cutter (I use my biscuit cutter).*

*Bake at 400° F. 'til lightly browned.*[71]

Buxom Dolley definitely had a sweet tooth. She declared, "I derived my pleasure from my indulgence." One of her indulgences was her own Dolley Madison cake served with hot bouillon laced with sherry.[72] Not all was sweet in Dolley's diet, even though the famous couple could be said to resemble Jack Sprat and his wife (President Madison weighed barely 100 lbs. and measured 5 feet 4 inches tall). Dolley immortalized him as "the great little Madison."[73] (It has been written "that America's greatest contribution to western civilization is the thinking of James Madison," father of the Constitution and architect of the Bill of Rights.)[74]

One of Dolley's specialties was spoonbread.[75]

## *SPOON BREAD*

*2 c. corn meal*
*2 c. boiling water*
*3 large tbsp. butter, melted*
*1 tsp. salt*
*1 1/2 c. sweet milk*
*3 eggs*

*"Sift the meal three times and dissolve in the boiling water, mix until it is smooth and free from any lumps. Add the melted butter and salt. Thin with the milk.*

*"Separate the eggs; beat until light; add the yolks and then the whites. Pour into a buttered baking dish and bake in a moderate oven (350° F.) about 30 minutes.*

*"This should be served in the dish in which it is baked."* [76]

It was during the Madison presidency that the peculiar War of 1812 broke out. The conflict with England has been called the Second Revolutionary War because many of the same problems between the two countries were still smoldering. The war actually began two days ***after*** the British government announced that the Orders in Council (concerning shipping) would be repealed. These Orders were a major American grievance. Had our leaders known of this change the war could likely have been avoided. The glorious final battle of the war which made Andrew Jackson the "Hero of New Orleans" occurred 15 days after the peace treaty had been signed. -- One of the effects of the war, besides resulting in the eventual election of Andrew Jackson (and William Henry Harrison) to the office of president, was the penning of "The Star-Spangled Banner" by Francis Scott Key. Key was inspired to write down his thoughts in rhyme as he witnessed the bombardment of Fort McHenry from a prisoner-exchange boat in Baltimore's harbor on the Chesapeake Bay.

During the war British Admiral Cockburn and his men entered the White House with destruction as the objective. However, Dolley had had the table set for dinner and the wine decanted before she received the message to flee (taking along Gilbert Stuart's George Washington portrait as she escaped). The invaders sat down to dine at the inviting table before setting the White House on fire.[77]

Even after the Madisons retired in 1817 to Montpelier, Dolley, the effervescent hostess, wrote of guests and big meals: "[We] had ninety persons to dine with us at one table -- put up on the lawn."[78]

The tastefully elegant Montpelier dining room was, of course, often the scene of the Madison's celebrated hospitality. This room, with gleaming wood floors and high ceilings, also served as one of the couple's four art galleries.[79]

Andrew Jackson was the seventh president. His wife Rachel had died just before Jackson took office. Before her death, though, the Jacksons had lead an active social life at their Tennessee mansion known as the Hermitage.

Rachel Donelson Jackson was born in Pittsylvania County (home of this book's author), Virginia. Rachel was the tenth child of Colonel John and Rachel Donelson. About the child it was said that she was "happy herself, and a source of happiness to all around her," [80] and that "those who knew her never tired of her beauty, her goodness, her sweetness and natural charm. She is described as being a brunette, with olive complexion and high coloring, black eyes that danced and sparkled in fun; vivacious and kindly." [81] Rachel was raised on a busy and prosperous Virginia plantation. She is described as having a wonderful memory for tales and anecdotes,[82] and as entertaining her nieces and nephews out in Tennessee by relating memories "of the elegant life back in Virginia, of the manners and customs, and of the fine ladies." [83]

As the wife of Andrew Jackson, Rachel was credited with the "admirable management of her household. In a throng of visitors she dispensed hospitality to all with cordiality." [84] Another accolade says, "She made a happy home, for besides being an excellent manager and mistress, she was kind." [85] Her beauty, executive ability, and other virtues caused one writer to declare, "She possessed those rare qualities which called forth the great love of a great man, which increased through the years, as her husband rose to fame and power. Few women in history have received so rich a meade [sic] of love and devotion." [86] Andrew Jackson himself added to the almost worshipful descriptions of Rachel: "We lived together, happy husband, loving wife, for nearly forty years. When I entered my room it seemed hallowed by a divine presence. I never heard her say a word that could sully an angel's lips. What I have accomplished I owe to her. . . . She made earth a paradise for me. Without her there could be no heaven." [87]

In the Hermitage, their Nashville home, the Jacksons were famous for their hospitality. Friends knew that they were welcome to honeymoon at the Hermitage, and many did so. The front guest bedroom there, in fact, has been called "The Bride's Room." [88] For the hungry honeymooners Rachel and her staff prepared restorative breakfasts and other palate-appealing meals. Andrew Jackson is said to have especially enjoyed chicken hash. Other Tennessee specialties might include "pork sausage, baked spare ribs, quail, grits, wheat bread, biscuits," [89] creamed eggs, fried ham and eggs and red-eye gravy, fried apples, and fruit-laden preserves and jellies.

## *"CHICKEN HASH"*

*2 tbsp. butter*
*1 1/2 tbsp. flour*
*1 c. chicken stock*
*2 c. chopped [cooked] chicken*

*"Make a white sauce with the flour and butter, using the chicken broth in place of milk. When thick, stir in chicken. Place in a buttered casserole and bake. Garnish with slices of toast."* [90]

## *"CREAMED EGGS"*

*5 hard cooked eggs*
*4 tbsp. butter*
*5 tbsp. flour*

*2 c. cream or milk*
*1/2 c. bread crumbs*
*Salt*
*Nutmeg*
*Paprika*

*"Make white sauce of butter, flour, and milk, season to taste with salt, nutmeg, paprika. Stir sauce until it boils.*

*"Slice eggs and place a layer in bottom of buttered casserole. Cover with layer of sauce. Repeat until filled. Top with bread crumbs, dot with butter, heat at 350° F. until warm."*[91]

### *"FRIED APPLES"*

*"Slice up apples and put in frying pan with a little water, cinnamon, sugar and a stick of butter. Fry until apples are clear."*[92]

### *RED EYE GRAVY*

*After frying slices of country ham, drain off the excess grease and add a little water to the drippings. Scrape the water and drippings together with a metal spatula and then add a tablespoon of strong coffee. Boil this liquid mixture and serve along with the sliced ham.*

# Chapter 3

# Frontier Foods

During the federal period Daniel Boone, John Chapman ("Johnny Appleseed"), and Lewis and Clark pushed westward, opening up new frontiers. These woodsmen and adventurers and other men such as Davy Crockett and Jim Bowie normally ate a diet different from the elegance of the White House cuisine which Jefferson, the two presidents Adams, Madison, Monroe, etc. were accustomed. Most food of the average man was wholesome and satisfying, though perhaps not elegant and fancy. However there are accounts depicting frontier cooking as less than appetizing:

> *"They eat salt meat three times a day, seldom or never have any vegetable, and drink ardent spirits from morning till night. They have not only an aversion to fresh meat, but a vulgar prejudice that it is unwholesome. The truth is, their stomachs are depraved by burning liquors, and they have no appetite for anything but what is highly flavored and strongly impregnated with salt."* [93]

(Daniel Boone's fame came in part from the fact that he was skilled at finding salt licks . . . .)[94]

Another negative comment (by an Anglican missionary in backwoods South Carolina) stated that the food was "exceedingly filthy and most execrable" and mainly made up of "clabber [thick, soured milk], butter, fat musty bacon, and cornbread." [95]

Happily, however, reports do exist of ample and enjoyable meals on the frontier. Game such as opossum, raccoons, venison, bear, wild turkey or other birds, rabbit, squirrels, wild cat, panther, and wild hogs made "good eating." Depending upon the locality, even buffalo (there were some herds east of the Mississippi early on), alligators, turtles, fish, and cormorants (large sea birds with webbed toes and a pouch under their beaks for holding fish) were consumed. Beaver tail soup was a tasty dish, although it tasted "too musky" in the summer.[96]

Poke salad and ramps (two types of greens) went well with cornbread. The forests yielded wild grapes and plums, berries, persimmons, apples, and nuts. The early frontierspeople who stayed in one place long enough planted vegetables such as corn, peas, beans, pumpkins, squash, and turnips. Corn, however, was the top priority became "a woman can take a . . . [hoe] in April and with a quart of seed plant a patch around a cabin and in six weeks she and her children can begin to eat roasting ears; and when it gets too hard for that she can parch it."[97]

Besides being a nourishing food corn could be made into whiskey. Early backwoodsmen had a reputation for guzzling grand quantities of spirits if there seemed to be no immediate danger of Indian attack, etc. Alcohol was used as both stimulant and tranquilizer, anesthetic, disinfectant; and drink of hospitality. Even babies were given weak toddies to calm them. Blackberry wine and persimmon beer were brewed. Drinkable water and milk were not always available, so alcoholic beverages seemed a logical choice.[98] A joke describes a "Kentucky breakfast" as consisting of a big beefsteak, a quart of bourbon and a hound dog -- the dog eats the beefsteak.[99]

## *OPOSSUM*

*"The opossum is a very fat animal, with a peculiarly flavored meat. It is dressed much as one would dress a suckling pig . . ., removing the entrails, and if desired, the head and tail. After it has been dressed, wash thoroughly inside and outside with hot water. Cover with cold water to which has been added 1 cup of salt. Allow to stand overnight; in the morning, drain off the salted water and rinse well with clear, boiling water.*

*"Make a stuffing as follows: melt 1 tablespoon of butter in a frying pan and add 1 large onion which has been chopped fine. When the onion begins to brown, add the finely chopped liver of the opossum, if desired, and cook until the liver is tender and well done. Add 1 cup of bread crumbs, a little chopped red pepper, a dash of Worcestershire*

*sauce, 1 finely chopped hard cooked egg, salt and water to moisten. Stuff the opossum with the mixture, fastening the opening securely with skewers or by sewing. Put in a roasting pan, add 2 tablespoons of water and roast in a moderate oven (350° F.) until the meat is very tender and richly browned. Baste constantly with the opossum's own fat. When sufficiently roasted, take from the oven, remove the skewers or stitches, and put the opossum on a heated platter. Skim the grease from the gravy remaining in the pan; serve the gravy in a sauceboat. Serve with baked yams or sweet potatoes."*[100]

## *WILDERNESS RABBIT*

*1 rabbit, dressed and cut into pieces*
*1 c. flour*
*Salt and pepper*
*1 egg, beaten, plus 1 tbsp. water*
*3/4 c. dry bread crumbs*
*1/4 - 1/3 c. bacon drippings or lard*

*Mix the flour, salt, and pepper, and coat the pieces of rabbit with the mixture. Next, dip the pieces of rabbit into the egg and water; then coat in the bread crumbs. Brown the pieces in the hot fat in a large skillet. When nicely browned, slowly add 1 c. water and cover. Simmer for an hour or until tender. (Check occasionally, adding a little more water if necessary.)*

## *CABIN CORN PONES*

*4 c. cornmeal*
*1 tsp. salt*
*1 tbsp. butter, grease, or vegetable oil*
*1 1/2 c. boiling water (more or less)*

*Mix all ingredients, using enough water to make a workable dough. Form disk-shaped pones and place on an ungreased baking sheet. Bake at 400° F. for 10 minutes; then turn over the pones and bake 10 minutes more.*

### *"CRACKLING BREAD"*

*1 c. cracklings (diced)*
*1 1/2 c. corn meal*
*3/4 c. wheat flour*
*1/2 tsp. soda*
*1/4 tsp. salt*
*1 c. sour milk*

*"Cracklings are the pieces of meat remaining after the lard has been rendered from the pork. Mix and sift together the dry ingredients. Add the milk, stir in the cracklings. Form into oblong cakes and place in greased baking pan. Bake in hot oven (400° F.) 30 minutes."* [101]

Corn meal was for every day -- other flours were "for special."

### *BUCKWHEAT DROP BISCUITS*

*3 2/3 c. whole wheat flour*
*2/3 c. buckwheat flour*
*1 tbsp. baking powder*
*1/2 tsp. salt*
*3/4 tsp. soda*
*1/4 c. vegetable oil*
*1 1/2 c. (or more) buttermilk or sour milk*

*Combine the dry ingredients. Mix oil and milk and pour into the dry mixture, adding more milk if need be. Drop by spoonfuls on lightly greased baking sheets. Bake at 400° F. for 12 minutes or until done.*

## *HAND-WARMIN' BISCUITS*

*4 c. whole wheat flour*
*1 tbsp. baking powder*
*3/4 tsp. salt*
*3 tbsp. vegetable oil*
*Milk*

*Mix the dry ingredients. Mix the oil and 1 1/2 c. milk. Combine the dry things and the liquids, adding additional milk to make a spoonable batter. Drop by tablespoons onto lightly greased baking sheets. Bake at 425° F. around 12 minutes, or until the bottoms are golden brown.*

As the newcomers settled in the wilderness they began to bring in and breed farm animals. Hogs were easiest to raise, and poultry was enjoyed if it could be protected from predators. Cows for milk and meat added nourishment and variety to the diet. A working person's breakfast might include:

## *SAUSAGE GRAVY*

*1/2 lb. bulk pork sausage*
*1 tbsp. flour*
*1 1/2 c. milk or cream*
*Pepper*

*Crumble the sausage and cook in a large skillet, over low-medium heat. As it cooks break it up with a metal spatula or spoon. (Do not allow it to get too brown.) When the meat is done, pour off the excess grease, leaving about 1 tbsp. fat. (You do not need to be precise.) Stir in the flour, and gradually add the milk or cream, cooking until the gravy has thickened. (Use a wire whisk if necessary to avoid lumps.) Season with pepper. Serve over split biscuits.*

*Variations and notes: Some people make whole sausage patties and serve the gravy over them. Some folks use water instead of milk or cream in the gravy (sauce). Obviously the amounts of ingredients can be doubled, tripled, etc. for larger quantities.*

At a festive Christmas breakfast in Nashville pork sausage, baked spare ribs, quail, grits, biscuits and wheat bread, chocolate, and milk were served.[102] An 1837 dinner in Nashville consisted of rich soup with rice; boiled ham, roast beef, "two very large boiled fishes, elegantly cooked and served with creamed Irish potatoes, bread and pickles;" winter vegetables; cucumbers; pickled mangoes (muskmelon or cucumber); watermelon rind pickle; apple pie, custard pie; jellies and cakes; coffee, tea, and milk.[103]

Fried chicken was a delicious way to enjoy chicken, and Brunswick stew, too, used poultry or squirrel meat. For dessert pumpkin custard or blackberry bread were appealing.

### *"FRIED CHICKEN"*

*"Disjoint 2 young chickens. Dredge the pieces well with flour, sprinkle with salt and pepper and drop into deep fat. Fry until a golden brown. Brown small circles of cold mush (corn meal boiled in water with salt and poured in a pan until cold), and fry a dozen sprigs of parsley, to garnish the dish. Scald 1 cup of cream, add 1 tablespoonful of butter, salt and pepper to taste, and 1 teaspoonful of chopped parsley. Pour over the chickens and serve."* [104]

### *"PUMPKIN CUSTARD"*

*1 c. cooked pumpkin, fresh or canned*
*1 1/2 c. milk, scalded*
*1/4 tsp. salt*
*1/8 tsp. allspice*
*3/4 c. sugar*

*3 eggs, slightly beaten*
*1/4 tsp. nutmeg*

*"Combine pumpkin, sugar, salt, spices, and eggs. Add milk slowly, stirring constantly. Pour into well-oiled custard cups. Set in pan of warm water. Bake in moderate oven (375° F.) until an inserted knife comes out clean. Serve with whipped cream. 6 servings."* [106]

### *BLACKBERRY BREAD*

*"Stew blackberries and sweeten to taste. Butter some slices of bread, with crusts cut off. Then put a layer of buttered bread in the bottom of a serving dish and pour over it hot stewed fruit. Repeat until dish is full or fruit used. To be eaten cold with cream."* [106]

## CONCLUSION

Our culinary exploration of the Young Republic is ending, but the influence of those cooks, cookbook writers, and trend-setters of the early 1800's is still evident in today's menus and on our dinner tables. -- Yet we do not match the abundance (and wisdom) revealed in this 1835 letter written by Mrs. Priscilla Carrington Coles from Washington, D. C., to her young daughter Helen in Southside Virginia:

> *"We were invited to a great dinner last week and did not enter the dining room until candle light, when instead of meat and vegetables the table was covered with artificial flowers, pictures, oranges, sugar candy, nuts, wine and silver vases of hot water to set the plates on. We all took our seats and found a piece of bread wrapped up in a nice napkin, and a gold spoon*

*and a silver knife and fork by the side of all our plates. Presently they brought from the next room soup in plates and gave to everybody, then the plates were changed and we all had a piece of turkey and one kind of vegetable, and then some other meat and one kind of vegetable, and so they continued until the plates were changed 15 times for the meat course and twelve times for the dessert. Tell Cousin Green this and ask her if she does not think the people here are genteel.*

*"I tell you all this my child to amuse you, and not because I think such things can make us happy. I would . . . willingly have exchanged this fine dinner for a little fried bacon on a pewter plate, provided it could have been eaten with my dear children."* [107]

## NOTES

[1] Laurel Elizabeth Hicks, *New World History and Geography in Christian Perspective*, A Beka Book Publications, Pensacola, FL, 1982, p. 252.

[2] Philip Kopper, "On the Manner of Their Feasting," *Colonial Williamsburg*, Winter 1988-1989, p. 9.

[3] Mary Tolford Wilson, "The First American Cookbook," 1958, Oxford University Press, Inc., essay in a facsimile of Amelia Simmons, *American Cookery*, reprinted by Dover Publications, Inc., Mineola, NY, 1984, p. *xvii*.

[4] Wilson, p. *xviii*.

[5] Amy Whorf, "At Home In a Colonial Kitchen," *Country Living*, December 1987, p. 140.

[6] Wilson, p. *xii*.

[7] *Ibid.*, p. *xv*.

[8] *Ibid.*, p. *xvii*.

[9] Washington Irving, "Early Life in Manhattan," reprinted in Walter Blair, Paul Farmer, Theodore Hornberger, and Margaret Wasson, *The United States in Literature*, Scott, Foresman, and Co., Glenview, IL, 1968, p. 170.

[10] Wilson, p. *xviii*.

[11] Simmons, p. 12.

[12] *Ibid.*, p. 13.

[13] *Ibid.*, p. 16.

[14] *Ibid.*, p. 10.

[15] *Ibid.*, p. 7.

[16] *Ibid.*, p. 46.

[17] *Ibid.*, p. 6.

[18] *Ibid.*, p. 46.

[19] *Ibid.*, p. 40.

[20] *Ibid.*, pp. 27-28.

[21] Karen Hess, *Martha Washington's Booke of Cookery*, Columbia University Press, New York, 1981, p. 313.

[22] Simmons, p. 37.

[23] *Ibid.*, p. 36.

[24] Carlotta C. Greer, *Foods and Home Making*, Allyn and Bacon, New York, 1931, p. 321.

[25] Vivian Minor Fleming, "Lafayette Ginger Bread," pamphlet, Washington-Lewis Chapter, D. A. R., Fredericksburg, VA, 1924.

[26] Joe Gray Taylor, *Eating, Drinking, and Visiting in the South: An Informal History*, Louisiana State University Press, Baton Rouge, 1982, p. 107.

[27] Henry Haller with Virginia Arosen, *The White House Family Cookbook*, Random House, New York, 1987, p. 234.

[28] James A. Bear, Jr., "The Hemings Family of Monticello," *Virginia Cavalcade*, Winter 1986, pp. 81-82.

[29] *Ibid.*.

[30] *Ibid.*, p. 79.

[31] *Ibid.*, p. 82.

[32] Marshall Fishwick, "Thomas Jefferson," *American Heritage Cookbook*, American Heritage, New York, 1964.

[33] Marie Goebel Kimball, Ed., *Thomas Jefferson's Cook Book*, Garrett and Massie Publishers, Richmond, 1949, p. viii.

[34] Haller, p. 248.

[35] Camille Glenn, *The Heritage of Southern Cooking*, Workman Publishing, New York, 1986, p. 256.

[36] Patrick Dunne and Charles L. Mackie, "Clio's Table: Herbal Mystique," *Historic Preservation*, May-June 1991, p. 82.

[37] *Sauer's Basics*, Vol. 1, No. 5, C. F. Sauer, Co., 2000 West Broad Street, Richmond, VA.

[38] Haller, p. 259.

[39] *Ibid.*, p. 256.

[40] *Ibid.*, p. 267.

[41] Fishwick, pp. 138-139.

[42] Haller, p. 5.

[43] Louise Conway Belden, *The Festive Tradition: Table Decoration and Desserts in America 1650-1900*, W. W. Norton & Co., New York, 1983, p. 5.

[44] *American Heritage Cookbook and Illustrated History of American Eating and Drinking*, American Heritage Publishing Co., Inc., New York, 1964, p. 139.

[45] Kimball, p. 26.

[46] *American Heritage Cookbook*, p. 139.

[47] Fishwick, p. 139.

[48] Hess, p. 26.

[49]Haller, p. 153.

[50]Frederick Herman, "An Unusual Survival," *Virginia Cavalcade*, Summer 1978, p. 15.

[51]Mary Randolph, *The Virginia Housewife (1828 Edition)*, quoted in Frederick Herman, "An Unusual Survival," *Virginia Cavalcade*, Summer 1978, p. 15.

[52]Mary Randolph, *The Virginia Housewife (1824 Edition)*, quoted in Haller, p. 367.

[53]Mary Randolph, *The Virginia Housewife (1824 Edition)*, quoted in Jonathan A. Zearfoss, Editor for the Virginia Chefs Association, *The Great Chefs of Virginia*, The Donning Company, Norfolk, VA, 1987, p. 112.

[54]Patrick Dunne and Charles L. Mackie, "Clio's Table: Cookery Books," *Historic Preservation*, May/June 1990, p. 58.

[55]Hess, p. 6.

[56]*Ibid.*, p. 6.

[57]Haller, p. 191.

[58]Zearfoss, p. 142.

[59]*The Cliveden Recipe Book* (from historic Cliveden, Germantown Avenue, Philadelphia), published by the Preservation Press, National Trust for Historic Preservation, Washington, DC, 1976, p. 15.

[60]*Ibid.*, p. 21.

[61]*Queen Anne's Table*, Edenton Historical Commission, Edenton, NC, 1976, p. 47, recipe contributed by Mrs. John Gilliam Wood.

[62]*Ibid.*, p. 39, recipe contributed by Margaret Davis.

[63]*Ibid.*, p. 93, recipe by Pauline C. Shepard (1885), contributed by Mrs. John Graham.

[64]*American Heritage Cookbook*, p. 138.

[65]Haller, p. 365.

[66]*Ibid.*, p. 365.

[67]Karen Clark, "Ice Cream," *Philip Morris Magazine*, July-August 1990, p. 32.

[68]Haller, p. 365.

[69]Alice Curtis Desmond, *Glamorous Dolly Madison*, Dodd, Mead & Company, New York, 1946, pp. 174-175.

[70]Haller, p. 32.

[71]Recipe courtesy Epps Perrow, Hurt, VA. She comments, "My old kinsman would come back to haunt me if I called this a recipe for 'cookies!'"

[72]Haller, p. 34.

[73]Kim Keister, "Montpelier Reconsidered," *Historic Preservation*, November-December 1991, p. 41.

[74]*Ibid.*, p. 34.

[75]Haller, p. 100.

[76]Lillie S. Lustig, S. Claire Sondheim, and Sarah Rensel, Editors, *The Southern Cook Book of Fine Old Recipes*, Culinary Arts Press, Reading, PA, 1939, p. 31.

[77]John Whitcomb and Claire Whitcomb, *Oh Say Can You See: Unexpected Anecdotes About American History*, William Morrow and Co., adapted for use in "Test Your Political I. Q.," *Country*

*Living Magazine*, November 1988, p. 46.

[78]Taylor, p. 62.

[79]Keister, p. 83.

[80]Maud Carter Clement, *Turn of the Wheel: Sketches of Life in Southern Virginia 1756-1956*, p. 30, reprinted in *Writings of Maud Carter Clement*, Pittsylvania Historical Society, Chatham, VA, 1982.

[81]John Trotwood Moore, *Jackson and His Beloved Rachel*, quoted in Maud Carter Clement, *History of Pittsylvania County, Virginia,* 1929, p. 157, reprinted by the Pittsylvania Historical Society, Chatham, VA.

[82]Clement, *Turn of the Wheel*, p. 35.

[83]*Ibid.*, p. 30.

[84]*Ibid.*, p. 27, quote attributed to "Benton."

[85]*Ibid.*, p. 35, quote attributed to "Parton."

[86]Unnamed Jackson biographer, quoted in Clement, "Turn of the Wheel," p. 26.

[87]Clement, *History of Pittsylvania County, Virginia*, p. 157.

[88]Jean W. Liles, Ed., *The Southern Heritage Family Gatherings Cookbook*, Oxmoor House, Birmingham, AL, 1984, p. 111.

[89]Taylor, p. 54.

[90]Lustig, Sondheim, and Rensel, p. 12.

[91]*Queen Anne's Table*, p. 72, recipe by Mrs. Hurley Winborne.

[92]*Ibid.,*, p. 73, recipe by Mrs. Cabel Pruden.

[93]Thomas Ashe of England, commenting on Kentuckians' diet upon his visit to Bardstown, quoted in Morris Bishop, "Louis Phillippe In America," *American Heritage* April 1969, p. 93.

[94]*Ibid.*, p. 48.

[95]Taylor, p. 20.

[96]*Ibid.*, p. 8.

[97]*Ibid.*, p. 11.

[98]*Ibid.*, p. 13.

[99]Lustig, Sondheim, and Rensel, p. 47.

[100]*Ibid.*, p. 16.

[101]*Ibid.*, p. 31.

[102]Taylor, p. 54.

[103]*Ibid.*, p. 57.

[104]Kimball, pp. 72-73, recipe attributed to Mrs. Mary Randolph.

[105]Ida Migliario, Editor, *The Household Searchlight*, *The Household Magazine*, Topeka, KS, p. 142, recipe contributed by Mrs. Herbert Kleis, Lackawanna, NY.

[106]*The Spinning-Wheel Cook-Book*, The Spinning-Wheel Club, Woodville, MS, 1899, reprinted 1939 by the Methodist Missionary Society, Woodville, p. 36.

[107]Clement, *History of Pittsylvania County, Virginia*, pp. 204-205.